CHASING SMOKE:
A Bucket List of the South's
Best Barbecue

J. Kent Thompson

ISBN 978-1-387-13842-5

Copies can be ordered from the publisher at:

www.lulu.com\shop\

1st Paperback Edition

Share your favorite barbecue places and any comments; contact the author @ jkt416@gmail.com

TABLE OF CONTENTS

Foreword

To Sam, my son and barbecue "Tour de la Que" companion.

FOREWORD

This a is a book about finding the best barbecue in the south. Now, I know that is a tall order. I also know some people will not agree with my choices but, if that is the case, they can research and write their own book.

Historically the barbecue world has been divided up into regions, each with their own cuts of meat and special sauces. I can appreciate that, and what you do with the meat after it is cooked can give one a different perspective. But I am coming from *how* you cook the meat. If it is not done right, you can always hide it under some different spices, or with some sweet, mustard, vinegar, or pepper sauce. Then you add some coleslaw, and say it is the best thing since sliced bread. My goal was to find out who cooks it the best, and how they did it. To find out, I have visited over fifty different barbecue restaurants from Texas to the Carolina's. I have tasted their food, looked at their pits, and spoke to the pit masters. Many of the places I visited are recognized nationally in magazines and on television, and listed as the "10 Best" or "50 best", or are bucket list places "you have to try before you die." Some lived up to the hype, some did not. To begin, let me tell you what I was looking for, that way, if you go try them out, you will know where I am coming from.

Barbecue is not cooking on a grill in the backyard. It is not cooking meat on an electric oven/smoker using pressed wood pellets. Barbecue is *slow cooking meat with indirect heat from the coals of a wood fire that infuses the meat with the flavor of its rendered fat and the smoke.* And that my friend, is what I have set out to find. I hope you enjoy the trip.

It all started in March of 2016 with an email. My son, Sam, sent me a bucket list of barbecue places you _must_ visit in your lifetime. I thought about it for a while, day dreaming about what a neat trip it would be to go visit each one. Then I thought, "Why not?" I called Sam and said three words that were to change two dry, hot, summers into a culinary adventure, "Let's do it!" Sam is an administrator at a local school and has the summers off, so he quickly agreed. The list included many well-known BBQ places in Texas, Kansas City, Missouri, Memphis, Tennessee, as well as Kentucky, Alabama, Georgia, and North and South Carolina.

We met to map out our trip. The first decision was what to call our trip. Sam suggested the "_Tour de la Que._" Our next consideration was where to go, and how best to get there. Barbecue is done differently depending on what part of the country you visit. We knew that Georgia was known for good pork, Texas for brisket, Kansas City for wet ribs, Memphis for dry ribs, and the Carolina's for whole hog and chopped pork. We chose to avoid Kentucky's mutton.

With this in mind, we developed our strategy. For our summer of 2016 trip we decided to rent a car and drive to Atlanta, Ga for our first leg and then travel by plane from Atlanta to Austin, Texas. From Texas, we would fly to Kansas City, Missouri, then Memphis, Tennessee, then free-lance it by rental car through the Carolina's back to Florida. For the 2017 trip we decided to drive the entire way, starting in Alabama, then Georgia, North Carolina, South Carolina, then back through Georgia, to Florida. We started both trips the week after Father's Day. It was extra special to me to be able to spend it with Sam on the "Tour", extending that special day into an extra week.

It was agreed to split the expenses, with one buying the airline tickets and meals, and the other the hotels and rental cars. We figured we would need five rental cars, eleven hotels, and three airline flights. We choose the Southwest Airlines "just get away" one way flights from Atlanta to Austin, then Austin to Kansas City, and finally Kansas City to Memphis. As it turned out the flight to Kanas City involved a flight change in Denver, and the flight to Memphis required a change in Dallas, so we added two more cities to our travels (if only temporarily.)

The flights, hotels, and cars were all reserved by April. We started researching barbecue places in each city. I had recently bought two good books on historic southern barbecue. One was _Smokestack Lightening_ by Lolis Eric Elie, who chronicled the whole hog barbecue of the Carolinas and Georgia. The other, _The One True Barbecue_ by Rien Fertel was a homage and follow-up to the former, with a modern-day writer retracing the search. Fertel had grown up in the restaurant business, but appeared to have little prior knowledge of real barbecue.

I spent time on the computer researching what others said was the best barbecue. I looked at their "Top Ten" and "Top Fifty" lists of barbecue place in the south. I copied maps of the North and South Carolina Barbecue Trail's. I put a post on Facebook telling friends about our trip plans and requested suggestions of places to visit. Many recommended the well-known places in the "Top" lists. While I took it all in, I knew that regardless of the well-known, there were some places out there that were local institutions waiting to be discovered. One of our goals was to go to the old historic barbecue places around the south that cooked on wood fired pits, not the ovens using wood pellets that dominate the restaurant business today. I compiled a list of places we could go in each of the cities we planned to visit, and prepared to travel.

ONE   GEORGIA

Sam and I picked up our rental car and headed to Atlanta. Our plan is to hit a favorite Atlanta barbecue spot for dinner, spend the night near the airport, then board a plane the next morning for Texas.

Our first destination was *Fox Brother's Barbecue* on 1238 Dekalb Avenue NE in Atlanta's Little Five Points district. We arrived right at five o'clock and the place was packed. The small parking lot was full and our first obstacle presented itself—where to park? As if the barbecue gods heard our plea, a car parked right in front of the business pulled out of their parking place giving us a front door spot. I knew right then this was going to be a good trip.

We parked and went in the restaurant. It is a former garage converted to accommodate the hungry customers. Tables were filling up, though the ones on the porch out front were still empty. As we were seated, I noticed a brisk take-out business, people were lining up to get their orders and hurry home with their barbecue. The waitress came and took our order. We decided to try their sampler plate of pulled pork, brisket, ribs, jalapeño sausage, and wings. We also ordered their sides of Brunswick stew, brisket chili, mac and cheese, and collards. We asked that any sauce be delivered on the side so we could first taste the meat before it was influenced by any additives. To wash it all down we ordered sweet tea. Hey, it is the south what else is there to drink?

When the plates arrived, we began a ritual that would take us through our trip. First, we took a picture of the food, divided it up so we both had a sample of all the offerings, said grace, then began tasting them one at a time. After each sample, we would discuss its good and bad points, later, when back at the hotel, we would rate them on a scale of 1 to 10.

Fox Brothers Atlanta, Ga

So how did Fox Brothers fare? We liked the waitress, she was good in making menu suggestions and the service was excellent. The sauce was a little strong with a Worcestershire flavor, more like a steak sauce taste. The brisket was fair, tasting more like a roast than good brisket. The pulled pork was spot on. It had a good bark, little fat, smoky flavor and good pull. The wings had been first treated with their rub, a little spicy but pleasing to the tongue, then sauced. The taste was very good. The ribs were disappointing. They had little smoke in the meat and the rub was a little overpowering. The jalapeño sausage was not what I expected, it had little jalapeño heat and the cheese inside just made it taste mealy. Our reaction to the sides was mixed. While the mac and cheese was excellent with a hearty cheesy flavor balanced just right, the Brunswick stew was a little too sweet and otherwise bland. The brisket chili was flavorful and good tasting, too bad the brisket we ordered was not. The collards were only average. They definitely know how to make a good strong, sweet tea like I am accustomed to. Over-all we came away from Fox Brothers with some good impressions.

We returned to the hotel stuffed full of barbecue. To top off the night (and week) we were able each night to have either a NBA championship series game or a NCAA Baseball World Series game to watch on television, heaven was smiling on us!

Because we had planned to travel to Texas from the Atlanta airport, we delayed the rest of our Georgia barbecue sampling until we were free-lancing back south from the Carolinas. Upon our return to Georgia we hit a few of their well-known places.

B's Cracklin' Barbecue Savannah, GA

I had heard of B's and knew they did whole hog, so we looked forward to tasting their Georgia fare. We were not disappointed.

B's had been through some rough times; his first business had burnt down right after he started gaining a reputation for good barbecue. After a short while, he opened a new place in a strip mall. The inside was decorated in wood paneling and pictures of the original building before and after the fire were displayed.

We ordered the brisket, pork, ribs and chicken. Our sides were mac and cheese, collards, baked beans, and hash (if you don't know what it is---don't ask.)

The plates came out steaming hot off the smoker, giving off a sweet smoke smell. It was served with a ketchup/mustard sauce on the side that was flavorful. The brisket had a good bark and taste, but still needs a little work to be top-notch, but it is not far off. The pork was excellent. B's nailed the smoke flavor and melt in your mouth goodness. The ribs matched the pork— great! It pulled off the bone and had a good pork flavor that was seasoned just right. The smoked chicken was smoky goodness. The sides were good. The beans had a good flavor, the collards were cooked and seasoned well, and the mac and cheese had a good cheese flavor. The hash was not bad either. Served over rice, it had a unique flavor that could be pleasing if you did not think of its ingredients. We washed it down with southern sweet tea made like momma used to make. We also ordered some banana pudding, which was excellent.

Inside the new B's Cracklin' BBQ

Southern Soul Barbeque St. Simon's Island, Ga

Southern Soul has the right atmosphere. License plates from around the country are nailed on the exterior. A sign proudly brags about all the magazine writers and TV shows that have visited and drooled over their fare. More importantly, six *Lang* smokers sit outside chugging out smoke, filling the air with the aroma of wood smoke barbecue.

A converted filling station, it has long wooden tables arranged outside for guests to sit family style. You share your space with whomever sits beside you. For this trip, taken Memorial Day weekend 2017, I took my best friend Jim with me, promising to show him some good barbecue. Sam still had teaching responsibilities, we would get together after classes ended.

We ordered the two-meat special that comes with a side of Brunswick stew, another side of your choosing, and two packs of saltine crackers. We chose brisket, ribs, turkey and chicken. Sides were mac and cheese, and French fries. We ordered sweet tea to wash it all down.

We sat down at a table and in a short ten minutes, a tattooed waitress called our names and brought the plates over. The food looked good, but there was no smell of hot meat. Obviously, what we were served had not come off the smoker recently. I tried the brisket. It had a pretty smoke ring, but was dry. It had a bitter smoke flavor and was closer to roast beef than brisket, what a disappointment. Next, I tried the ribs. The rub was sweet and tasted good, but the rib was fatty without a good smoked meat taste, or pull. The chicken had the same rub as the ribs. It was a thigh and breast together. The thigh was moist (it has more fat in it and should be) but the breast was too dry. The turkey had no flavor at all.

On to the sides. The Brunswick stew had too much vinegar in it that consumed the meat flavor inside. The mac and cheese was good, but salty. They offered four different sauces, I found the Georgia Hot to be the best, the others were not to my liking. Maybe it was just a bad day for Southern Soul, but it was the Friday before Memorial Day, and it should have been better.

They have the right smokers, but either they are not being cleaned regularly, or the cooks don't know what they are doing. There is no excuse for such sorry barbecue off a *Lang*. After such a disappointing meal, I told Jim I would take him somewhere I knew had good food. I decided to take him to B's Cracklin' Barbecue in Savannah. At the least, I could show Jim the difference between the meal what we just had, and good barbecue.

Back to *B's Cracklin' BBQ*

We were waiting for the Savannah restaurant to open at 11:00 the next morning. I took Jim around back to look at B's smoker, it too was a *Lang*. We walked in to the sweet smell of barbecue smoke and placed our order. I ordered ribs and brisket, Jim ordered brisket. The night before in our hotel room I had showed him a clip from Arron Franklins TV show on how to cook brisket. He now had a better idea of what to look for in good brisket.

B's Cracklin' did not disappoint. For sides we ordered collard greens, hash, and mac and cheese. A cornbread muffin came with the meal as well as a cup of his sauce. Everything was washed down with good sweet tea. The sauce was a spicy mustard mixed with a little ketchup to give it a red color.

Jim saw the difference in what we had been served at Southern Soul and B's Cracklin' immediately. B's brisket was moist and broke apart easily. It had a good smoke ring and even better smoke flavor. The last time I came to B's I had said he was on his way to good brisket and this was closer to the best I have had in Texas. The ribs had a good pull, with great flavor. They had a salt and pepper rub. The sides were excellent. The collards were cooked just right, and the cheesy mac and cheese was like momma made. The cornbread was good too. I did not care for the hash, as it was smothered in their sauce, and the vinegar was a little heavy. The meat in it was good, but too much sauce. All-in-all, it was well worth a second trip to B's. I got to enjoy great barbecue a second time and Jim learned a little about the nuances of *good* barbecue.

Sprayberry's Bar-B-Que Newnan, Ga

Sprayberry's has been a family owned and operated business since 1926. The old barbecue pits are still in view outside the store, having been abandoned due to age and modern health department regulations. Country music star Alan Jackson used to wait tables here, and Atlanta columnist/humorist Lewis Gizzard has a sandwich special named after him. We ordered one of their famous pulled pork sandwich's. The pork was dry, but when you added in one of their two sauces, it tasted good. Of all the different sauce's we were to taste on our two trips, I would have to say Sprayberry's Original Recipe sauce, and their mustard sauce, were some of the best we had.

Heirloom Bar-B-Que Atlanta, GA

Hidden away beside a grocery store on Akers Mill Road is a barbecue restaurant with a Korean twist, the Heirloom Market. We pulled into the cramped parking lot and maneuvered for a parking spot.

Diners can choose to take-out (which due to limited parking, many did), or stand at tables in the patio area to eat. We ordered ribs, brisket, and chopped Korean pork. Sides were glazed sweet potato chips and kimchee.

The brisket was cooked well, but needed more salt and pepper for flavor. The chopped pork was well cooked and flavorful, seasoned in a Korean style. The ribs reminded me of Southern Soul BBQ as they had the same rub. They were good enough. The sides were different for an ole country boy, but the glazed sweet potato chips were interesting. I drew the line at the kimchee, letting Sam have that. He said it was good. Heirloom is drawing a lot of attention in the Atlanta area and their twist on barbecue is different, but good.

Community BBQ Atlanta, Ga

Community BBQ is located in a strip mall beside other interesting places to eat. We ordered their chicken, ribs, and pulled pork. For side's we got mac and cheese, greens, baked beans, and coleslaw.

Everything that came off the smoker at Community BBQ was cooked to perfection. The pulled pork had a good infusion of smoke and was moist, not dry. The ribs had a good pull, but I found they tasted like barbecue chicken. The chicken was excellent! It had good smoke and was moist. Their two sauces, one sweet and the other vinegar, complemented the meats well. The coleslaw was fresh.

The baked beans were a little undercooked and had too strong of a coffee taste. The greens were well cooked and tasty. The mac and cheese was a hidden delight. It was infused with butter and cheese and tasted like heaven. You cannot go wrong with anything on their menu.

Old Brick Pit BAR-B-Q Atlanta, Ga

The Old Brick Pit Bar-B-Q looked like a hometown favorite. Though it advertised being in business since 1976, the young Vietnamese woman running the place was probably not the original owner. But I will say, they have kept the tradition alive. We ordered ribs, pulled pork, Brunswick stew, slaw, and fresh peach cobbler. The ribs were very good. They were infused with smoke and flavor. The pulled pork had good smoke, and was moist, not dry. The slaw and sauces good. The peach cobbler was homemade goodness.

Moonies Texas Barbecue Flowery Branch, Ga

Moonies was recommended by a friend and I am glad I took her up on the recommendation. Located in the city where the Atlanta Falcons hold their football training camp, it is a diamond in the rough. The owner came from Austin, Texas and introduced Texas style barbecue to this corner of Georgia. When he first opened, he kept the doors open until the meat was gone. But the locals, not used to such a business model, begged for longer hours. It was obviously a good decision, as I watched cars fill the parking lot on the day we visited. We ordered brisket and pork sandwiches, both had great smoke and flavor. Both of the sauces offered complemented the meats. Moonies is the real deal if you want Texas style barbecue, they do it right.

Wiley's Championship B-B-Q Savannah, Ga

When visiting Savannah, I had asked a hotel consigliere to recommend some good barbecue places to eat. She said Wiley's and Sand Fly were two popular places, but she preferred Sand Fly. We were waiting at the door when Wiley's opened. We ordered a pulled pork sandwich and ribs. The meat was cooked well, but lacked any smoke flavor. The ribs were only so-so. The sauce tasted like it came from Sonny's barbecue. Needless to say, it was a disappointing trip. We decided to try Sand Fly next.

Sand Fly Bar-B-Q Savannah, Ga

When we got to Sand Fly, it had been open about a half an hour and a line was formed at the counter. Looking at the menu we were surprised to see that in addition to brisket, pork, and chicken, they offered duck fat fries and white truffle fries. We ordered the pulled pork sandwich. It had great bark and a good smoky flavor. It was cooked to perfection. While it was good enough to eat without sauce, we tried their two offerings, both were great. This is definitely a good place to get barbecue in Savannah.

TWO   TEXAS

We flew in to Austin, Texas, eager to try some of their barbecue.

We decided to go directly to Lockhart, Texas, about 16 miles out of Austin to try some of the famous barbecue at three well-known establishments, Smitty's, Blacks, and Kruez's. The drive out was interesting, as in Texas the speed limit on their interstate is 85 miles an hour. It took no time to get to Lockhart. We decided to try Smitty's first.

Smitty's Market Lockhart, Texas

Entering Smitty's is stepping back into time. From the outside, it looks like an old brick storefront. Walking through the door you encounter a long hallway that is filled with the blue haze of sweet smelling smoke. To the left is a door to an old meat market and counter, down the hall a wood fire is burning, standing beside the fire is a friendly middle-aged pit-master signaling you to come on in.

We walked up the hall and immediately felt the heat of the log fire, its smoke was being drawn into huge brick pits covered by steel doors. The pit-master raised the doors and exposed grates full of brisket, ribs and sausage, slowly smoking. "Lord", I thought, "just let me live here the rest of my life." My nostrils were filled with the sweet smell of barbecue, my skin and clothes infused with smoke— I knew I had entered barbecue heaven.

We were ushered to a counter behind which stood four men and a young lady. Behind them were more pits with exposed wood fires. The orders were pulled hot off the pit and wrapped in red butcher paper. After paying, the customers could either exit a side door, or go into the adjoining dining hall. The hall was filled with long communal tables adorned with napkin holders and a bottle of *Texas Pete* hot sauce.

The room radiated heat, with open fires burning next to your legs. All the workers were sweating and one was complaining that someone needed to come help them run the cash register.

We ordered ribs, brisket and jalapeño sausage. An extra helper came up to the complaining worker and he was quickly given a brief course in how to run the cash register, "Just put in the amount, tell them what it is, take their money and give them the change, don't worry about counting it back to them," he was told.

One important thing we were to learn on this trip was that many barbecue places are a _cash only_ business, so don't expect to bring a credit card and get fed. I must admit, we were excited. Here we were in Lockhart, Texas, famous for its barbecue, getting ready to sit down and eat our first bite of Texas barbecue. We paid for our food and went into the dining hall. There was a counter to the right where you could order sides of onion or jalapeño peppers, plus a stack of white bread to eat with your meat. We chose not to try the sides, but got glasses of water.

We sat down to try the brisket, ribs and sausage. The brisket came in either lean or fat cuts and we had slices of each. I should note that in Texas they serve meat by the pound, but we found that you can also order by the slice or number of ribs. The lean brisket had a good smoky beef flavor and the fat slice was even better. We tried the ribs next, and to be honest, I was surprised at how good it tasted.

I had expected good beef in Texas, but not pork. It, like the brisket, had just the right mixture of salt and pepper seasoning augmenting a great smoked flavor. It kind of surprised me that the "silver skin" was still on the back of the ribs. At home, I pull it off to make an easier eating rib, but as we progressed through our tour we found this to be the case at many barbecue places. Probably the skin was left to make the cutting of the ribs easier.

Texas also has beef ribs, huge dinosaur looking things, but we decided to forego them. To us it was more like eating pot roast on a stick. The jalapeño sausage was next. It was good, but hot! So hot, I needed to refill my water glass. I had recently tried some jalapeño sausage a friend had brought back from Texas and I expected some of the same flavors, but this sausage was just hot. It missed the sweet heat of a good jalapeño sausage. We finished our food and headed up the street to Black's.

Black's Barbecue Lockhart, Texas

Black's looked like you would expect an old-time barbecue place to be. Outside the rustic wood exterior, was a short waiting line. For the convenience of their customers, there was a water cooler to refresh themselves as they waited. Old 60s country music tunes were playing over a loudspeaker, and people chatted amiably while they stood in line.

After a short wait, we entered a walkway lined with photos of politicians and dignitaries of Texas past who had visited Black's. I noticed that copies of the same photos were gracing the wall on the other side of the restaurant as well.

The line offered a view of the interior where people sat eating barbecue at red-checkered tables. The line queued toward the front, passing a woman offering sides to be purchased before you ordered your meat. None looked too appetizing, so we skipped them, instead concentrating on the meat. We ordered our meat--- lean and fat brisket, and pork and baby back ribs. Sitting down at our table, I noticed a slight grease film on the plastic tablecloth adding to the ambiance of the place. Posters and neon signs advertising Texas beer hung on the walls. A display offered tee shirts and hats with the Black's logo, as well as bumper stickers that said, "*The only two places to eat: Black's and Home.*"

We greedily tried our second plate of food for the day. The lean and fat brisket was cooked well and the portion was a thick cut. It was seasoned with salt and pepper. The pork ribs were good, but the baby backs were only fair. Unlike Smitty's, Black's had a sauce to go with their meat. It was an interesting sweet tomato flavor. We finished our food and went out down the street to Kruez's Market.

Kruez's Market Lockhart, Texas

Kruez's Market is both new and old. The current location is the result of a family split. Its owners used to be associated with Smitty's, but in 1999 they opened their own business in a new location. To maintain their history of being in business since 1900, a pan of fire coals was drug through the streets of Lockhart from Smitty's to the new Kruez's Market.

The new Kruez's is a huge building, visible as one comes into the city of Lockhart. Because of its location it probably attracts more business than Smitty's or Black's. We noticed that Black's had erected signs pointing to their location in an attempt to steer customers their way. Smitty's however had no such sign's and I kind of understand the implied logic— *"if you don't know about us"* they seem to say, *"then you don't know good barbecue."*

But after witnessing the disarray of their counter operations, it also might be that they just aren't as business savvy.

A long line was waiting when we came into the huge parking lot. After parking, we obediently fell into line. As we waited you could see that one half of the building (where it was minimally air conditioned) was filled with diners, while an open-air half stood empty. Signs adorned the walls. One gave a list explaining the service to the uninitiated: "*No Barbecue Sauce (nothing to hide), No Forks (They are at the end of your arm), No Kidding (see owner's face), Just the best barbecue and sausage we can make.*"

A man standing behind me pointed out a huge rattlesnake hide framed on one of the dining hall walls. Sam noticed the etching on a glass door that read: "*Vegetarians enter here, normal people down the hall.*" We soon edged up to the front of the line where you could see the pit's. The pit-master open one to reveal rows and rows of sausage cooking, on another were ribs and briskets. The room was smoke filled and fires were burning at the base of the pits, just like Smitty's. Unfortunately, the newness of the building took away from the ambience that one encountered at Smitty's.

We ordered brisket and ribs but decided to forego the sausage. While those in Texas may like the sausage, to us it was just filler, not barbecue. The brisket came in fat and lean slices with the fat slice having a better taste than the lean, though both were a little heavy on the salt. The ribs had a good smoke to them but once again the heavy salt took away from the enjoyment of the meat. Served with the meat was your choice of white bread or crackers.

We decided to return to the hotel to rest up from eating three meals and to choose a place for dinner.

We chose *Stiles Switch Barbecue and Brew* which was rapidly gaining a reputation in the barbecue world.

Stiles Switch BBQ and Brew Austin, Texas

Stiles Switch BBQ and Brew is named after the historic I. & G. N. railroad stop in Stiles Switch, Texas. It is in Lamar's Violet Crown Shopping Center, one of the oldest shopping centers in central Austin. It was also the film production hub for the late 1990s film "Dazed and Confused" starring Matthew McConaughey. Their restaurant space is the famed "Emporium" pool hall, filmed in the movie.

Walking in to the restaurant, we instantly got the feel that this was a local favorite. Families were sitting at the tables and lining up to order their meals. We got in line and ordered their two-meat special. By doing so we could order four different meats and sides, then share. We chose brisket, turkey, pork loin, and ribs. The sides were coleslaw, potato salad, hominy with green chilies, and cheese and corn casserole. We also ordered some banana pudding. I got a soda to drink and Sam got sweet tea.

The food is served on a white porcelain tray etched with a blue border, giving one an old-time restaurant feel. The brisket, turkey and pork loin were all seasoned well and tasty. The ribs had a good rub on them, and good smoke. *Stiles Switch* offers two types of sauce, a sweet and flavorful vinegar sauce, and a mustard sauce with a hint of horseradish in it, giving it a strong flavor. Of the two I preferred the vinegar, but the mustard was good. The coleslaw was very good, only outpaced by the potato salad with a sour cream base that made it taste great. The corn casserole was a little dry. The hominy with chilies and cheese was just ok. The banana pudding dessert was the real deal! It had a good mixture of pudding, banana's and vanilla wafers. Over-all *Stiles Switch* had a good atmosphere and a good meat selection that, regardless of what you ordered, you would be satisfied.

Having been to four barbecue restaurants in one day we decided to call it a day. Our bellies were full of brisket and ribs to the point that we had to re-evaluate how we were going to manage this "Tour de la Que" to the end.

The next day we had a special treat planned—we were going to *Aaron Franklin's Barbecue.*

We got up early and decided to try a little something different—doughnuts—for breakfast. I had noticed the famous *Round Rock Donut* shop was only about twenty minutes out of Austin and suggested we try it. *Round Rock Donuts* had been featured on some Food Channel shows as the home of the "*Texas-sized*" donut. It is a huge yellow batter donut that could easily feed a family. *Franklins* would not open until eleven so we decided to go out to *Round Rock* then come back to Austin to *Franklin's*.

Famous Round Rock Texas-Sized Doughnut

When we arrived at the donut shop there was a line of car's in the drive-up and a line inside the store. We found a parking place and went inside. The display cases were filled with all types of delicious looking donuts. A girl behind the counter took our order, gave us a number and said they would glaze our donut, then have it ready (you could get either chocolate or regular glaze). Soon our number was called an we were presented with a large box, the size you may put a sheet cake in. Inside was one huge glazed donut. We sat outside and started eating our donut. While we ate, people walking by would gawk and point at the size of the sweet round of glazed dough we were eating. It took about fifteen minutes, but we managed to finish it off, quite satisfied with ourselves and quite full of donut. I would estimate that its size would collectively equal about a dozen donuts.

Franklin Barbecue Austin, Texas

We were excited to go to *Franklin Barbecue* because I had read his book and had been following him through his television show. *Franklin's* was famous for his brisket and we could not wait to try it.

In doing my research for the trip I gleaned a nugget of information that saved us a lot of time—you can pre-order your meat and avoid the lines. The only catch was there was a five-pound minimum order, prepaid a month in advance. One could order beginning the first Monday of the prior month only. I had made sure to put my order in the beginning of May, so all we had to do was show up a half hour before the place officially opened, walk to the front of the line, then go in and get our order.

We felt smug walking up to the restaurant where a long line stretched out of the parking lot to the street behind it. Going to the front of the line, I asked the couple in the very front, by the door, how long they had been waiting and they said "since 5:30 a.m." We went in and the waitress was busy filling orders and putting them in large grocery bags. I had ordered two pounds of brisket (1 fat, 1 lean),

1-pound turkey, and ribs. As an afterthought, I also ordered one of their small bourbon-banana pies. The pit-master cut and wrapped our order in red butcher paper. He then put it in a bag with a side of onions, pickles, a loaf of white bread, and two types of sauce. As we walked out of the restaurant, I noticed a look of hate from the couple waiting at the front door.

We went back to the hotel and unwrapped our food. The first thing to hit us was the smell of rich, smoky barbecue! We dove in to the meat. First savoring the melt-in-your-mouth tender brisket. It had a good salt and pepper bark and a beautiful smoke ring. The turkey had good seasoning and flavor. Once again, we were surprised by the good tasting ribs in Texas. The sauces were for dipping. One was a tomato/vinegar base with a citrus taste. The other was *Franklin's* own, a ketchup based coffee flavored sauce. I personally thought the coffee one too strong, but liked the tomato/vinegar. The pie was a delightful surprise. Made by *Cake and Spoon* in Austin, it had just the right mix of bourbon and banana. My only regret was that I had not ordered more.

Having finished the round of barbecue places in Lockhart and Austin, we felt we had a pretty good representation of Texas barbecue. Basically, Texas is all about the meat, seasoned only with salt and pepper, no sauce added, cooked over post oak wood coals low and slow. To me that is the hallmark of good barbecue.

We would find in our travels that many restaurants try to cover up their barbecue either with sauces, heavy rubs, or coleslaw, some successfully and other not so. But in the end, it's the way the meat is prepared and cooked that's the difference. We said good-bye to Austin, a great place for barbecue and a pretty town to boot, and prepared to travel to Kanas City for the third leg of our trip.

THREE   KANSAS CITY, MISSOURI

After a flight that routed us first to Denver, Co then to Missouri, we arrived in Kansas City and picked up our rental car, a white Toyota . Since we arrived a little later in the day, we decided to go to only one restaurant and chose Q39, touted as a happening place.

Q39 BBQ Kansas City, Missouri

The parking lot was full and there was a line at the door. We finally found a place to park around back and went inside to find it would be a 15-minute wait. The place had a "yuppie" feel to it, not that of a barbecue place.

It was crowded and we were ushered to a small table located between other diners. The crowd was friendly and the noise was tolerable, even though everyone was close. We ordered the two-meat plate's so we could taste a variety. We also ordered an appetizer of wings.

The wings came first and were presented with sauce and a sprig of parsley on top. They had a fair taste but seemed more grilled, then covered with sauce. The sauce was sweet and had a peppery flavor. We both agreed the sauce hid the meat flavor. Our order of ribs, chicken, pork, and sausage arrived. For sides we had coleslaw, potato salad, beans with burnt brisket ends, and white beans with sausage. A piece of cornbread came as well. All were about the same—more grilled than smoked, with the flavor hidden under sauce. The pork was a pork butt. It was not chopped well, and the muscle tube fibers in it were tough. The slaw was plain and sweet, and the other sides uneventful. The cornbread was fluffy and looked promising, but lacked taste. We were not impressed, and noticed that besides barbecue they served seafood and salads. Warning to the barbecue connoisseur—if they serve anything but barbecue, they probably don't do good barbecue. Another thing to watch out for is barbecue sold in airports—really...?

We checked into our motel and called it a day. That night we reevaluated our approach to trying so many restaurants at one time and came up with a better plan.

We decided we would go to as many places as we felt would represent the cities barbecue and order what they were best known for. We would then bring it back to the hotel, and one by one, try it and do our rating. This would eliminate sit-downs in the restaurants and allow us to go more places.

We decided to ask for the selections with whatever sauce or slaw they provide on the side, so we could judge the meat without any other flavor interference. Any bread would also be taken off. After we had judged the meat, we could then taste the over-all product with the additions to see its combined flavor. But hey, we were on a quest for the best barbecue—not the best sauce, bread or coleslaw.

Danny Edward's Boulevard Barbecue Kansas City, Missouri

Today we implement our new strategy—go to as many representative places, then return to the hotel to taste. First up was *Danny Edward's,* located but a mile or so from the Kansas-Missouri border. The current store is new having been built after the former downtown store was forced out by the city development. Formerly known as *Lil' Jake's,* it had a reputation for good take-out, as seating was limited. They even developed a motto of "*Eat it and beat it."* A pink pig adorned the outside of the building.

The wait staff are friendly and helpful. The place is known for its burnt end brisket sandwiches, so we ordered one to go, plus a pulled pork sandwich. Both came on fresh buns with the sauce on the side. The burnt ends were flavorful with a good smoke crusted char. The pulled pork had a good smoke infused flavor. The sauce, made with a vinegar/tomato base was weak and ineffective.

Gates Barbecue Kansas City, Missouri

Gate's has four stores in Kansas City, we went to the one on Brooklyn Ave. Driving up to the store we noticed everything in the surrounding shopping centers are named *Gate's* something—florists etc.

The store looked promising, smoke was pouring out of the roof and when we walked inside we were engulfed with smoke. The service was lunch counter style with a line moving up to the food. A woman called out to us with, "What do you want?" We ordered and waited. After standing there for about ten minutes she asked us again, having forgot what we ordered.

Another few minutes passed and finally the pulled pork and sliced pork sandwiches we ordered were presented. We asked for some sauce on the side and she said it cost's extra. Now *Gates* is supposed to be famous for their sauce so I found it hard to believe they would not give you any for take-out. I noticed a sauce counter on the way out so I got a small cup to taste their sauce. It was a tomato flavored sauce, infused with Tabasco and pepper. If this was their famous sauce, I think I will just pass. The sandwiches were bland at best and the sauce overwhelmed the taste of the meats. This coupled with the poor service did not impress us much.

Joe's Kanas City Bar-B-Que Kansas City, Missouri

Joe's is famous for starting up in a gas station. It is still there and the BP gas station does a brisk business.

The restaurant was packed when we went in. A line formed, and we took our place. I noticed a grocery shelf to our left packed full of all types of barbecue sauces and rubs, even from *Joe's* competitors. We ordered a pork sandwich and ribs. To drink we ordered sweet tea. Upon tasting the meat, the first thing that struck us was the lack of smoke in the meat. This coupled with little flavor in the pork disappointed us. The ribs had a rub applied that was ok, but once again there was no smoke or flavor to the entry. They had two sauces, regular and spicy. The regular was thick, spicy, and sweet and tasted like something you could buy off the shelf. The spicy sauce was the same taste only hotter. *Joe's KC Barbecue* was all sauce and no smoke. The tea however was sweet and good.

Arthur Bryant's Kansas City, Missouri

We went to the original *Arthur Bryant's* store on Brooklyn Ave. To enter you walked into a small foyer with a gate on it. A picture of Arthur adorned the wall. Inside we were greeted with a good smoke smell. We ordered a pulled pork sandwich and ribs. Our order was wrapped in butcher paper and presented to us. The ribs had a pork flavor but little smoke. The pulled pork had a good pull but some of their sauce (which was too sweet) was on it so you could not taste the meat. I had heard Kansas City was all about the sauce and after *Gate's,* and *Joe's,* and now *Bryant's*, I was beginning to see that it was true.

S.L.A.P.S. Squeal Like a Pig BBQ Kansas City, Missouri

S.L.A.P.S. motto is "*Squeal like a pig.* There was limited parking in front of the old red building. It seemed inviting, like a real barbecue joint. We entered to a small seating area with a counter on the side, to order. We ordered a pulled pork sandwich and ribs. The pork had a sweet flavor and the ribs had a good pull off the bone. They both had good smoke in them. *S.L.A.P.S.* offers two types of sauces, the first was sweet and reminded me of teriyaki sauce. The second was tomato based and reminded me of plain hot sauce. After the disappointment of the prior three places, *S.L.A.P.S.* was a welcome change.

Jack Stack Barbecue Kansas City, Missouri

By the time we thought about trying *Jack Stack* we felt we had a pretty good handle on Kansas City barbecue. We did go into the restaurant and looked at the menu—they serve seafood and salads... The decor was dark and it looked like an upscale restaurant, not a barbecue place. I am sure that many are brought to *Jack Stack* to taste Kansas City barbecue since it is the most centrally located, but that does not particularly equate to good. I asked a few people who had gone there and one said, "They have great corn!" Enough said. If I am slighting you Jack Stack, send me some and I will give you a try. But I bet it is more of the saucy Kansas City same.

B-B's Lawnside Blues and Barbecue Kansas City, Missouri

For our last barbecue meal in Kansas City we decided to go off the beaten path. I am not suggesting that *B-B'S Lawnside* is not one of the recognizable places in Kansas City, just that you have to travel to get there—but it is worth the trip.

We drove out to the restaurant in the evening just before the night's entertainment was to start. Tonight, it was the Nick Schnebelen Band. From the building's exterior, it looks like a local's place and that was confirmed when we went inside. After paying the $5.00 cover charge for the blues band playing, we were seated at a long row of tables adorned with a plastic red checkered tablecloth. We ordered our food just before the band started playing. We ordered pulled pork, ribs, and chicken with a fried tater plank on the side. We also ordered some of their bread pudding for dessert.

The music started and put everyone in a friendly, foot-stomping, hand-clapping mood. The male and female lead singers belted out some great blues to the crowd's enjoyment. *B-B's* is supportive of local bands, with some playing return engagements monthly.

The food came out and we started tasting. The pulled pork tasted sweet, but was lacking good smoke. The ribs however, were great. The meat had a good bark and was fall off the bone. The chicken was well cooked and had a good smoke flavor. They had a good sauce, light but not overpowering. The bread pudding alone is enough reason to go back. It was fantastic, on the same dessert level as *Franklin's* pies. All in all, a good friendly atmosphere, good food, and a great band.

FOUR   MEMPHIS, TENNESSEE

Today we said good-bye to Kansas City and boarded a plane for Memphis, Tennessee. After a trip by way of Dallas, Texas we arrived in Memphis just at dinnertime.

We circled our Hampton Hotel on Beale a couple of times looking for a place to park. I finally went inside while Sam circled again to find out how to get to their parking garage. Once parked we checked in and decided to take a walk down Beale Street ala the song *"Walking in Memphis."*

It was Wednesday night and apparently that is bike night for the locals. Motorcycles of all sizes and shapes were lined up, with their owners flashing their colors and club jackets while standing around talking. We looked at all the neon signs and storefronts, some with blues music blaring out the doors. Sam spotted a restaurant (one of the few non-bar places on the street) called *Miss Polly's Soul City Cafe*. We decided to go in and get a bite to eat, as it had been a long day of airline travel.

The restaurant was decorated with posters of blues greats with some superimposed on the tables. On the wall over the entrance to the bathrooms was a sign stating: *Love, Peace and Chicken Grease Let's All Get Sancti-fried.*"

We got a menu, ordered some sweet tea and tried to decide on what to eat. While I was looking at the menu I took a big swallow of the tea—Whoa! I definitely was back in the south. The sweet tea tasted like a mouthful of honey.

We decided to order the fried chicken and waffles. They came to the table hot with the waffle topped with melting butter. The chicken was moist and juicy and had a good fried skin that had a taste of hot sauce in it. I later asked the chef about it and he confirmed he soaks the chicken in hot sauce, par boils it, then fries it when ordered. It was great. The waffle was good tasting as well. We had ordered sides of mac and cheese and collards. Both were well cooked and seasoned. To top the meal off we ordered a fried apple pie in a skillet. It came to the table sizzling in a small frying pan with a melting dollop of ice cream on top. The dough was soft and sweet, coated in cinnamon, and the apples melted in your mouth. Though we did not have a barbecue dinner tonight, it was a good one.

We went back to the hotel and before going up to our room I asked the desk clerk if he could recommend some good barbecue places for us to go. He reeled off a few names of near-by famous offerings, but I pressed him saying "We want to know where *you* would go for the best Memphis has to offer."

Because I had relieved him of giving lip-service to the nearby places, he looked me dead in the eye and said, "*Payne's* or *Interstate.*" I asked him about another I had heard of called *A& R*, to which he replied it too was a good place. He then cautioned us saying "*Payne's* and *A& R* are in a little rougher neighborhood than downtown." I assured him we could take care of ourselves and really didn't plan on going into such neighborhoods to party at night.

The next morning Sam and I began our ritual of going to as many places as possible then coming back to the hotel to taste our bounty. Our first stop was *A & R Barbecue*.

A & R Bar-B-Que Memphis, Tennessee

A & R stands for Arthur and Rose, the proprietors. Their restaurant is located in the Hickory Hill area of Memphis in a converted store. We rolled up about 10 minutes before their 10 a.m. opening and waited. Once the doors were opened we went in and ordered.

The staff was a little disorganized but we counted that to some just arriving for work. We ordered a chopped pork sandwich and ribs. They top their sandwich with slaw so we asked for it on the side as well as the sauce. One thing we noticed about the slaw in Memphis, it is finely chopped and has a mustard base as compared to the coarser chopped and mayonnaise based slaw we were used to eating.

Waiting for the sandwich and ribs, we noted the newspaper article posted on the walls touting Kevin Hart's visit to the store. He stated that while he was visiting, the future King and Queen of England were also visiting at another uptown restaurant named *The Rendezvous*. He stated he doubted they would make it down to *A& R*. Too bad, they missed it.

We got the sandwich and left for our next restaurant. In retrospect, I wish I had checked the bag—they had left out the ribs and had instead given us two chopped pork sandwiches. So instead of tasting the ribs we were limited to the chopped pork. It was moist and full of good smoke and had a sweet taste that was pleasing. The slaw was nothing to write home about, but the tomato based sauce was sweet and spicy.

Payne's Bar-B-Que Memphis, Tennessee

Payne's is another place identified as being in a rough neighborhood, and they are right. But it is worth the trip. We arrived before the 11:00 opening time and waited. A man in a black Cadillac waited next to us. A few minutes before 11:00, the man got out holding a $100.00 bill in his hand, eager for it to open. Soon the door was unlocked and we walked into a dimly lit, smoke filled room.

Behind the counter stood a man with a gun on his hip, a teenager collecting the money (cash only), and an old woman chopping pork. Soon more people came in and lined up behind us. It seemed everyone knew when the place opened and were hurrying to get their barbecue before he ran out. I might mention we were the only two white people in the place but that did not really matter.

We ordered a pork sandwich and two ribs. The owner must have misunderstood us because he gave us a pork sandwich and two rib sandwiches. But that was ok.

The ribs were on a bun covered with the yellow slaw of Memphis. We took off the slaw and tasted the ribs, they were delicious! The meat pulled off the bone and was full

45

of smoky goodness. Same for the pork. It had a good chop and had flavorful bark included. The slaw itself was sweet and tasted good. Out back of the building, the smoke poured out of a chimney calling all barbecue enthusiasts to some excellent barbecue.

Interstate Barbecue Memphis, Tennessee

We went to *Interstate*, as recommended by our hotel clerk. While he had the first two recommendations right, *Interstate* was a fail.

We walked in, and right away noticed the almost black, dirty ceiling tiles, made more noticeable by the recent replacement of one new, bright, white one.

We ordered ribs and a pulled pork sandwich. While waiting we looked around and saw ceramic pig busts, tee shirts and sauces for sale. I am beginning to think that those who want to sell anything but barbecue in their restaurants are trying to deceive you into believing their food is good.

We got the sandwiches and ribs. The ribs were fall off the bone and had a smoky taste but overall were bland. The pulled pork was drenched in a sauce and while moist, was nothing special. The slaw was peppery flavored and unimaginative.

After tasting the selections from all the afternoon's restaurant's, we picked our winners and kept the selections from *Payne's* and *A & R*.

For dinner, we decided to try the well-known barbecue place in downtown Memphis just a couple of blocks from our hotel, *Charlie Vergo's Rendezvous*.

Charlie Vergo's Rendezvous Memphis, Tennessee

We walked to the restaurant, located in the middle of the block with an alley-way entrance. The place was full of diners and we were seated quickly. The waiter took our order of ribs and pulled pork with a side of mustard slaw and baked beans.

We eagerly awaited the famous Memphis style dry-rub ribs. When they came, it looked like a dry rib with Italian seasoning on it—very heavy oregano flavor. The ribs were cooked crisp, not fall off the bone. but the seasoning was terrible. The pulled pork was even worse. The only good things on the plate were the beans and the sauce. We figured the sauce had to be good to cover up the taste (or lack of taste) of the meat. The slaw had a spicy and pepper flavor. The sauce was the thick sweet sauce type you can buy in the store. It seems that the best way to eat the food is to cover it with sauce. As a matter of fact, that goes for Memphis barbecue (excluding *Payne's* and *A & R*) just cover whatever you cook with sauce and people will like it—but it's not real barbecue. Memphis should stick to the Blue's for its reputation, that's something there is no doubt about!

The next morning, we decided it was time to free-lance a little and wander through Alabama and the Carolina's in search of good barbecue. We left Memphis in our rental car, another Toyota. I can see why they use them as rentals, they get phenomenal gas mileage.

Before we left Memphis, we had to try their well-known doughnut shop, *Gibson's* that promised the best donuts around.

We went into a crowded store where four or five people were behind the counter taking orders. The problem was the people they were waiting on were standing in front of the donut display, so you could not make a selection.

We ordered some glazed donuts, a maple bacon donut, two jelly-filled donuts, and two cups of coffee. We sat down at a table near one that housed some obvious regulars, who the owner was entertaining.

He was telling of a singer that had visited the night before and how he was on the roof tossing donuts to a large crowd that followed him there, thanks to social media. We tasted the glazed donuts touted as better than *Krispy Creme* and found a light donut that was nothing special. Surely *Johnson's Bakery* in Perry, FL is much better. The coffee was poor quality and we decided to toss it. So much for *Gibson's Donuts*.

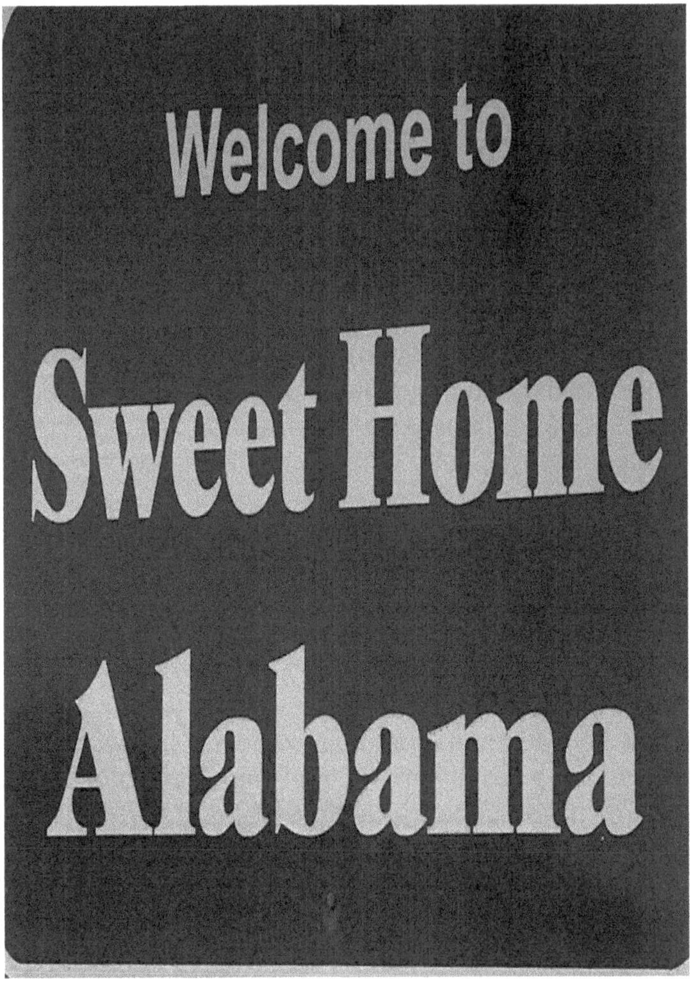
Welcome to
Sweet Home
Alabama

FIVE   ALABAMA

There are many restaurants in Alabama that have been in business for years, and each one we tried had an indoor wood fired pit. We were to find out that most of the good barbecue in Alabama consisted of chicken, cooked in pits over wood fires. That was a good thing. We found few that could cook good ribs, and that most of the sauces were terrible, which was a bad thing.

Big Bob Gibson Bar-B-Que Decatur, Alabama

We decided to head to another place with the same name as the donut shop, *Big Bob Gibson's* in Decatur, Alabama to try his famous chicken and Alabama white sauce. We arrived at *Big Bob's* at lunch time and the tables were full of tourists and families. The entrance way displayed old, dusty BBQ trophies, and the overall look of the place was tired. Most of the waitresses were middle-aged and had probably been with Big Bob for years. They were friendly and efficient.

We ordered a plate of chicken, ribs and pork. When the food came out you could not see the white sauce on the chicken as I had been led to believe you could. On closer inspection, I found some in the crevasses of the chicken and on the bottom of the plate.

The chicken was excellent. It was cooked well and had a good smoke taste. It appeared to be seasoned with salt and pepper which was tasty. The sauce however was too vinegary. The pork was terrible. The ribs pulled off the bone and had a rub and sauce applied that was ok. The rub had a little heat in it, but the sauce was too strong and tasted like Fritos. We had a side of beans and mac and cheese, but both were unappetizing. I ordered a homemade coconut cream pie, and while it presented well, the custard filling was a little runny, otherwise it was good. I would recommend anyone going there to skip everything but the chicken—it's worth it.

Miss Myra's Pit Barbeque Birmingham, Alabama

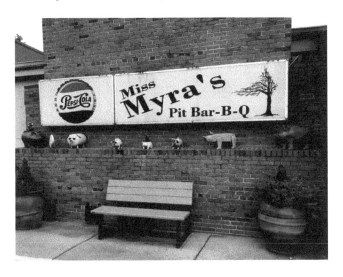

Miss Myra's started business in 1984, cooking on their indoor brick pit. We ordered the chicken, ribs, beef brisket, and pulled pork. Our sides were green beans, potato salad, baked beans, and collards. Miss Myra's ribs and chicken were great, having good smoke and taste. It was some of the best barbeque ribs and chicken on the trip. The white sauce had too much of a vinegar taste and the red sauce was blah. You really don't need it for the chicken or ribs. Because the beef and pork were dry, one might want to hide it with a sauce. The vegetables were bland, having a buffet type limpness. The potato salad was the one standout. A treat at Miss Myra's was their homemade desserts. Great pies, and the banana pudding was fantastic. Best in Alabama.

Bob Sykes BBQ Bessemer, Alabama

Before we went to Bob Sykes, we watched a video he had produced about his restaurant. It was very convincing, he spoke of the purity of meat cooked over wood, infused with smoke. He told the family history and their years in business and how they had started with the chicken and later added ribs. After watching the video, we were excited to taste Bob Sykes food. Like other heritage barbecue sites, Sykes had an indoor brick pit where you could see the wood burning and your meat cooking. We ordered the chicken, ribs, and pork. For sides, we got the mac and cheese, potato salad, and baked beans. For a dessert, we got lemon pie and red velvet cake. The waitress told us it would be a forty-five-minute wait for the ribs, but we were ok with getting fresh cooked ribs. Imagine our surprise when the plates were delivered fifteen minutes later, and everything was drenched in red, spaghetti tasting sauce. The ribs were of poor quality, needing to be cooked longer. The pork was dry and overcooked, a result of being on the grill too long. The chicken however, was excellent, as was the mac and cheese. The potato salad was bitter, with too much vinegar. The beans looked like they were right out of the can. The lemon pie and red velvet cake were excellent. All in-all Bob Sykes did not live up to the hype. They should stick to the chicken and desserts. The other meats were over sauced, and the meal was generally overpriced.

Dreamland Bar-B-Que Tuscaloosa, Alabama

Dreamland recently opened a restaurant in the Tallahassee Mall so I skipped the detour to the original. If they are going to become a chain, they need to represent wherever they are. Dreamland is known far and wide for their ribs, so the bar was set high going in. The Tallahassee, FL restaurant has an inviting atmosphere and is capable of seating many. When we went, we were the only ones in the place. We ordered ribs, pulled pork and pulled chicken. Sides included mac and cheese, baked beans, fried okra, and coleslaw. Sweet tea was ordered to wash it all down.

The pulled pork was from a Boston Butt, which was a little too fatty, though it had a mild smoke flavor. If covered with their sauce, it tasted good. Next was the chicken. It was tender and tasty. The ribs had a good smoke flavor and a slight char that added to the flavor. The sauce was a good compliment to them. The side of okra was delicious, as was the coleslaw. The mac and cheese was tasteless macaroni in Velveeta cheese, and the beans were out of the can. The sweet tea is pure southern sweet tea, like eating sugar, which I enjoyed. *Dreamland* has a good pork rib, even though that type of rib tends to be fatty. Their sauce goes well with the meat. If you go, get the ribs, slaw, and okra. Forget the rest.

Our final thoughts on Alabama barbecue is that they use the right materials, brick pits, wood fires, fresh meat. But generally, they are better at cooking chicken than pork. But hey, who can't cook chicken? Save for the ribs at Miss Myra's and Dreamland, Alabama and pork barbecue don't mix.

SIX   NORTH CAROLINA

North Carolina is proud of their barbecue history. It is in North Carolina where one can still find barbecue cooked the real way, in a wood-fired pit. The state divides its barbecue up by two types; Eastern that uses a vinegar-based sauce, and Western that uses a ketchup based sauce, also called "Lexington" style locally. In speaking with an eastern Carolina pit-master he explained that "in the east we show you are meat, and it stands alone, while in the west, they hide it with red sauce." Another thing we noted about North Carolina whole-hog barbecue is that it is served finely chopped. When we scouted out places in North Carolina, I wanted to make sure we went to some of the old historic pits. The North Carolina Barbecue Society puts out a listing of their locations, so we chose four; Bridges, Skylight Inn, B's, and Wilbur's.

North Carolina Historic Barbecue Pits

Skylight Inn- Ayden
B's Barbecue- Greenville
Jack Cobb & Son- Farmville
Wilbur's –Goldsboro
Grady's BBQ- Dudley
Stephenson's- Willow Spring
Allen & Sons- Chapel Hill
Stamey's- Greensboro
Short Sugar's-Reidsville
Hursey's- Burlington
Carolina BBQ- Statesville
Herb's-Murphy
Red Bridges-Shelby
Switzerland Cafe- Switzerland
Salisbury
Little Richards
Wink's

Winston-Salem   **Lexington**
Hills   Speedy Lohr's
Little Richards   Smiley's
                                    Bar-B-Q Center

Bridges Barbecue Lodge Shelby N.C.

Bridges has one of the historic pits in North Carolina, having been in business since 1946. They specialize in pulled pork sandwiches. We each ordered a sandwich and some banana pudding. We drank some excellent sweet tea as we waited for our order. The sandwich did not look appetizing on the plate. It was grey. It had no taste. The sauce was pure vinegar. All I can say for Bridges is they might have been good, but no longer can they rely on a name. Only the sweet tea and banana pudding were worthwhile. It was after eating at Bridges that we made a decision on North Carolina pulled pork. We had planned to go to Lexington to check out some of their renown barbecue, but then had to ask ourselves, did we want to spend the next two days eating pulled pork sandwiches? The answer was no, had one, had them all.

We instead headed to Asheville, NC. I had called ahead for a reservation and we checked into the hotel around 6:00. I asked the desk clerk for any barbecue recommendations and he quickly said you have to try a new place just down the road called *Bonfire Barbecue*. We entered the address into our GPS and headed to *Bonfire*.

Bonfire BBQ Ashville, North Carolina

I knew I was going to like the place when we drove up and saw a cardboard cut-out of Dale Evans welcoming us at the front door.

The waitress greeted us and showed us to a booth. The place is comfortably decorated with sports on tv, a bar, and an adjoining pool hall. On the far wall is a blue NC flag with a star and *"Bonfire- Est 2015"* displayed. When one goes to the bathroom they are greeted by a cut-out of Dale's hubby Roy Roger's, the *"King of the Cowboy's,"* pointing the way.

We ordered the two-meat with two sides meal. The meats were ribs, brisket, pork and wings. The pork had a good flavor and the ribs had a good pull. They had a good

59

smoke, chew, and a good rub applied. The wings were smoked then fried, and while they were good, hid the smoked flavor. They offered all their meats straight -up which we respected. The owner, Jeff, stopped by our table and we told him we liked his place and food, while filling him in on our current barbecue adventure. He told us he is trying to improve daily and working with his pit staff to increase their cooking knowledge. He apologized for his brisket, saying it was not quite where he wanted it, and we had to agree. It was fair, but with a little more coxing, was going to be great.

Bonfire had something we had not seen in any other barbecue restaurant so far—a sauce bar. Jeff felt it was best to let the meat speak for itself, then if you wanted to add sauce, go for it. He was a man after our own hearts! The bar had six different choices; western North Carolina (tomato & vinegar), *Bonfire* (spicy), Eastern (vinegar), KC Honey (sweet tomato), Barnburner (extra hot), and South Carolina mustard. What a great idea! I especially liked the South Carolina Mustard and the KC Sweet. The sides were collards, cooked and seasoned just right, and baked beans that had a coffee flavor from the blackstrap molasses that had been added. We also tried the mac and cheese, which was good but needed more cheese to rival Atlanta's *Fox Brothers*. Not offered as a regular side but included with their lamb special for the night were some feta and rosemary grits. Sam especially enjoyed them while I found the feta a little strong for my taste. We washed it all down with some good southern sweet tea. I ordered the apple crisp for dessert and it was very good. If you are looking for good barbecue in Asheville, *Bonfire Barbecue* is the place!

We left Asheville and headed towards Eastern Carolina to find some of North Carolina's whole-hog barbecue in Greenville, NC. After a long drive, we pulled up to *Sam Jones Whole Hog BBQ*.

Sam Jones Whole Hog BBQ Winterville, NC

Sam Jones BBQ is in a relatively new building, but his history goes back to the *Skylight Inn* in nearby Ayden, NC. Sam has the new place, but cooks the old way. From the parking lot, we were drawn to the huge building that housed his pits beside the restaurant. The pit-master welcomed us in, and we were engulfed with the smoke as we entered. He raised the cover on one of the pits to reveal a 180lb. hog, slowly cooking over wood coals. Now here was the whole package—barbecue like it should be done. Not pieces of shoulders, butts, ribs, and hams, but the whole hog!

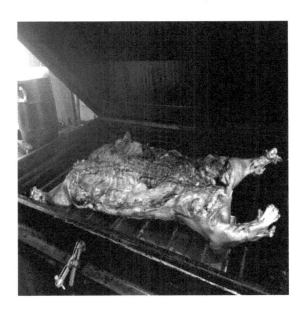

The smell was delicious. After walking through the glorious smoke-filled room, we went inside the restaurant. It looked new like every other buffet type restaurant, though it was not buffet.

We ordered a chopped pork sandwich and tasted some of the sauce bottled for sale. The sauce came two ways, sweet or vinegar, and both had a good flavor. The sandwich bun was toasted, which was different from any other place we had been. The slaw on the sandwich was finely chopped, but was a little too sweet tasting. The pork was the star. The meat had a full smoke flavor and was chopped perfectly. With *Sam Jones*, as well as the next two whole hog places, we would find that the meat almost melted in your mouth, it was so tender. Sam Jones was one place we went to on both trips. As a matter of fact, we were *jonesing* for some of that good whole-hog barbecue for a year. We were not disappointed; our second trip was even better than the first. Sam Jones does it right consistently. Our next stop was in Ayden, N.C. at the *Skylight Inn BBQ*.

Skylight Inn BBQ Ayden, NC

The *Skylight Inn, founded in 1947,* looks nothing like Sam Jones new restaurant. It has a roadhouse feel and the building is topped with a dome like the nation's capital. A sign outside says it all "*If it's not cooked with WOOD It's Not BBQ.*" I could not agree more; this place *is* the real deal. We walked in to see a man behind the counter chopping meat with two cleavers, one in each hand. The rat-a-tat-tat of the blades chopped the meat finer and finer as he piled and re-chopped it.

The *Skylight Inn* is like the barbecue places in Texas, they do a cash only business, no credit cards here. We ordered the chopped pork sandwich and a side of cornbread. It came out on a soft bun with the meat piled high. No sauce was on the meat, but a bottle of *Sam Jones BBQ Sauce* was available on the table. The chopped meat was infused with smoke and different portions of the hog. The cracklings had been added in, and the bits were visible in the meat. It tasted wonderful. The cornbread was good, not sweet but made the old-fashioned way with little baking powder. The Skylight was another place we visited twice. The second trip in 2017 saw a newer look interior to the place from 2016. It seems they decided to fix the place up with a new counter, tables and chairs. A display of barbecue sauces was offered as well as tee shirts. It seems like the Skylight has "gone Hollywood." The food was not as good on the second time around, while it was cooked well, it had a slightly more peppery taste than the first time, but it is still good whole-hog barbecue.

Wilbur's Barbecue Goldsboro, NC

Wilbur's has been around since 1962 and looked like what you would expect for a barbecue restaurant, kind of in the steakhouse style. A sign near the door said: "*WARNING YOU ARE ABOUT TO EAT THE BEST BARBECUE IN THE WORLD.*" They were right on in that respect. Like the *Skylight*, *Wilbur's* does a cash only business.

We were greeted by a friendly counter staff that took our order of a pork sandwich with the sauce and slaw on the side. The bun was the freshest and softest we had been served during our whole trip. The pork was full of a tangy, smoky goodness with the crackling's added in. It was by far the best whole hog pork sandwich I had ever eaten. The slaw was chopped cabbage, lime green and white, but not anything special. The sauce was pure hot vinegar. We tried Wilbur's again in 2017. This time we got served meat with the pepper and vinegar sauce already added. It was too hot to enjoy. My tongue tingled from the sauce, taking away from the enjoyment of the food. The meat was well cooked, they should not have ruined it with the sauce. We also were served hushpuppies with the meal, an eastern Carolina standard. They were good.

B's Barbecue Greenville, NC

B's Barbecue was a place we missed going to on our first trip. It opens early in the morning, so we were at the door at 9:00 in the morning. While B's cooks over a pit, there is a difference between them and the other eastern North Carolina pit masters. They cook over charcoal, not wood.

We ordered a pulled pork sandwich and gave it a try. Needless to say, it was disappointing. The entry tasted like a pork butt sandwich. Missing were the flavors of the whole hog. The sauce was straight vinegar. B's, in our opinion, is wasting good hog meat.

Bums B-B-Q, Ayden NC

We almost did not go to Bum's. It advertised a buffet and our first thought was you don't eat barbecue at a buffet. But we decided to give it a try, and I'm glad we did. The owner's son, Larry Dennis who runs the place now, was at the counter and welcomed us back to look at his new pits. He spent time explaining his set up and it was impressive. We went back into the restaurant and tried his whole-hog barbecue sandwich. It had great taste and a good smoke flavor throughout. Of all the whole-hog barbecue we were to taste, Bum's was one of the best. Coupled with Larry's friendly persona, Bums is the real deal. Don't go to Ayden without trying Bums. We left behind the smoking pits of Greenville, Ayden and Goldsboro, but their memory will be in our minds for a long time. Make no mistake about it, a plate of chopped whole hog barbecue is in a class all by itself. Until you taste parts of a whole hog, slow cooked for hours over wood coals, then chopped and mixed together, you have not discovered real barbecue.

Choose your Sauces and Rubs

SEVEN   **SOUTH CAROLINA**

On our first trip in 2016 we traveled in South Carolina on a Sunday morning, not a good time to find barbecue. We had planned to try some of the historic barbecue pits, but most are only open Thursday through Saturday. We made sure to adjust our 2017 trip to accommodate these days. South Carolina serves whole hog like the places in North Carolina with one difference, they pull the meat instead of chopping it. They also use four types of sauces; light tomato (basically pepper and vinegar with tomato added), heavy tomato which has sugar added for sweetness, mustard, and vinegar and pepper, all depending on which region of the state you are buying the meat. We chose to visit some of their historic pits, namely Henry's, Scott's, Hite's, Bessinger's, and Sweatman's.

Henry's Smokehouse Greenville, SC

Henry's Smokehouse was crowded when we walked in. The smell of hickory smoke filled our nostrils. We ordered a pulled pork sandwich and ribs with a side of mac and cheese and banana pudding. Both the pork and ribs were full of a good smoke taste. The ribs were a little overcooked and chewy, but tasted good. The pulled pork was tender and delicious. The mac and cheese was overwhelmed by the Velveeta cheese. The banana pudding was sweet, probably made out of canned vanilla pudding. Henry's red sauce was very good and complimented the meats. I asked the cook if I could come into his kitchen and was welcomed with the sight of a pile of Boston butts being prepared for the weekend. There must have been 50 on the prep table. Henry's delivers great Boston butts.

Pork butts being prepared at Henry's

Scott's Variety Hemingway, South Carolina

Getting to Scotts Variety BBQ takes dedication. Dedication to drive on poor South Carolina country roads 75 miles off the nearest interstate. When you arrive, it is not impressive, just a run-down country store beside the road.

Scotts started cooking hogs for the locals and their reputation blossomed. Today Rodney Scott has a fancy restaurant in Charleston where he charges $9.00 for the same sandwich we got in Hemmingway for $2.50. But that's what fame does and I am happy for him. Beside the store is a large Quonset hut type building where the hogs are smoked, and it is impressive. We ordered the pulled whole-hog sandwich and some pork rinds. We were to find that fresh cooked pork rinds are offered at all the South Carolina places we visited. We sat in the small store to eat. The meat was well cooked and as I said, pulled. While the meat was tender and well cooked, we did not like the fact that they had put sauce on the meat before serving it. It was light tomato, (basically vinegar and pepper sauce with a red color). Quite frankly it was too hot for my taste, really just pure Texas Pete hot sauce mixed in the meat. After a few bites, it was all we could take, which was unfortunate, we had expected better. If you like it hot, Scotts meets the bill, but to us it was too much. The pork rinds were delicious.

Hogs on the smokers at Scott's Variety

Hite's Bar- B- Que West Columbia, South Carolina

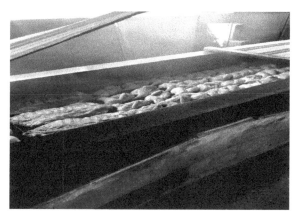

We visited Hite's on a Friday morning. The owners had just returned from a vacation to Florida and were busy cooking as they are only open Friday's and Saturdays. The owner took us back to look at his pits which were loaded with whole hog, ribs, chicken and pork skins. We ordered a pulled whole-hog sandwich. I was surprised to see it came with mustard sauce already added. The sauce was sweet and it made for a good sandwich, but the meat was good enough to stand alone. It was well cooked and had a good smoke flavor throughout. Hite's is definitely a place to go if in Columbia, S.C

Sweatman's Holly Hill, South Carolina

Sweatman's is located on an old dairy farm. The buildings that used to house the milk coolers have been converted to smokers. The old farmhouse serves as the restaurant. It was very impressive. We got there before it opened and walked around back to the pits. We were met by the pit master who invited us in to the smoke-filled rooms. On the fire were hogs and pork skins. He took the time to answer a few questions about cooking whole hog for us, then we left him to his duties. The doors opened a little early so we got to go inside. Sweatman's serves their food buffet style, and because they are only open two days, they sell out fast. You can buy individual meat to go, a one-time through the line plate, or an unlimited trip plate.

We got the one-time plate plus a pulled whole-hog sandwich. For side's we got mac and cheese, and greens. The meat was tender and well cooked, with good flavor. Once again, the meat came with the sauce added. It was a spicy-sweet mustard sauce, but I would have preferred to taste the meat without the sauce first. The ribs tasted a little too porky. The mac and cheese was good, like momma made. The banana pudding was out of can. Sweatman's cook's good whole hog, I just wished the sauce was separate.

Hogs cut in half and pork skins cooking

Fiery Ron's Home Team BBQ Charleston, S.C.

Home Team BBQ in North Charleston was packed with the lunch crowd when we stopped in. Right behind it is another barbecue restaurant called Lewis BBQ which, like Home

Team, is a happening place. Both are bringing Texas style brisket and barbecue to South Carolina. We ordered a sliced brisket sandwich to go with some mac and cheese on the side. The brisket was seasoned and cooked well with smoke throughout. The mac and cheese was just ok. One thing I liked about Home Team was their sauce offerings. Just like Bonfire in North Carolina, and Heirloom in Atlanta, there was a variety. One could pick the red, sweet red, hot red, mustard, vinegar, or the hot, hot sauce. All were good, especially because you add it yourself.

Bessinger's Bar-B-Q Charleston, South Carolina

Bessinger's is a family business opened in the 1960s. They have a reputation built on good barbecue and their gold mustard sauce. We were not disappointed. We ordered a pulled pork shoulder sandwich that was full of taste and good smoke. The sauces were very good. I preferred the mustard. The original hickory seemed to have too much of a liquid smoke flavor. Bessinger's and Sprayberry's sauces were the best sauce offerings we had on our trips.

Fresh Cooked Pork Skins

EIGHT   FLORIDA

Unfortunately, Florida does not have a great barbecue reputation. I guess it's because Florida is known more for its seafood than pork. But there are some good restaurants out there, you just have to look around. We chose two of some renown, Jenkins, and 4 Rivers Smokehouse.

Jenkins Bar-B-Q Jacksonville, Florida

Jenkins Quality BBQ has been in Jacksonville since 1957. There are three locations in town, we went to the one on N. Pearl Street. The store looks like an old hamburger joint converted to a barbecue restaurant, which it is. But there is a wood stack outside and a brick pit inside.

I have been going to *Jenkins* for years, always stopping for ribs during the Fla-Ga football weekend. The ribs are doused in *Jenkins* sweet mustard sauce, and you can't eat them without getting messy. But it is worth it. I can honestly say I have had better ribs, but *Jenkins* ribs are their own kind of special, and worth trying. They also serve a slice of red velvet cake that brings back memories of the way desserts used to be served in old time BBQ places.

4 Rivers Smokehouse Tallahassee, FL

4 Rivers Smokehouse is a relatively new barbecue spot in Tallahassee. The food is served up cafeteria style, you walk up and order what you want. I got the brisket, sliced both fat and lean. The meat was well seasoned. The fat piece had a little too much fat in it, the lean was ok. They had the best cooked brisket I have had in Tallahassee, but it could be better with a little more attention paid to the cook time. You can order sides (at an extra cost), I got mac and cheese and green beans. They were nothing special. The cornbread that came with the meal was a bit dry. They offer sweet tea and it was better than most. All-in-all it was an ok experience, but they are a little pricey.

Mission BBQ Tallahassee, FL

Mission BBQ opened a few months ago. I resisted going because I knew it was a chain restaurant, and usually the product suffers the farther you get away from the original. Finally, I took the leap. The store is nice, clean, and smells like smoke—that was a plus, but the food disappointed. I ordered a brisket and pulled pork combo plate with mac and cheese, green beans, and cornbread. To better evaluate the brisket, I asked for both fat and lean slices.

Both the fat and lean brisket was dry. Many accuse Florida Pit Masters of making brisket that tastes like roast beef— *Mission BBQ* fits that bill. The best way to eat it is to cover it with one of their six sauces. I tried the smoky mountain which tasted like regular sauce with liquid smoke added. The mustard tasted good initially -- until all the vinegar hits the back of your throat taking your breath away. The hot tupelo was neither. The pulled pork was moist, but lacked any real smoke flavor. While it had the taste of onion powder, it was bland otherwise. The mac and cheese was dry and lacked cheese. The green beans came out of a can with a piece of bacon added. The cornbread was probably the best thing on the plate, but it too was dry.

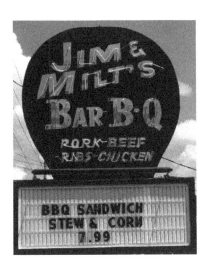

Jim & Milts BBQ Tallahassee, FL

Jim & Milts has been around for a long time. Their menu has changed little since it opened. Selling mainly to FSU students and the Tallahassee lunch crowd, they represent a filling meal at reasonable prices. The barbecue they offer, to the uninitiated is considered good. But then again, Ripple wine is too, if you have never tasted better. I ordered the lunch special which consisted of a fried ear of corn, Brunswick stew, and a pork sandwich served on garlic Texas toast, and sweet tea. The pork was cut thin and contained an edge of fat. It had little smoke flavor, the only way it was presentable was to cover it with the thin sauce offered at the table. The Brunswick stew was more of a potato in a weak sauce than anything else. The fried corn was good. The garlic bread was ok. The sweet tea was good. You get what you pay for.

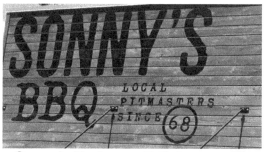

Sonny's Barbecue Tallahassee, FL

Sonny's is a home state favorite. They have expanded from small beginnings to a chain of restaurants all over the south. They offer up barbecue like *McDonalds* does hamburgers—you get the same wherever you go. For my family, they have been the go-to barbecue place for years. That is until I learned what real barbecue was.

We ordered the feast for four that included chicken, pork, ribs, and brisket. It came with choices for sides, so we got corn nuggets, mac and cheese, French fries, and baked beans. Eating at *Sonny's* is familiar, it does not disappoint in providing a fulfilling, cost efficient meal. But, the chicken was dry and the pork lacked any smoke, the brisket was good but tasted more like roast beef—but it was better than I had at *Mission BBQ*. If the *Sonny's* entry had the seasonings of *Mission BBQ* plus the cook time of *Sonny's*, they might make a passable brisket. The ribs had a good glaze on them but the ribs themselves were fatty. *Sonny's* saving grace for its meat is the sauces it offers, you can hide anything with a sweet sauce. All the sides were good, especially the beans and corn nuggets. The sweet tea was good. *Sonny's* is better than most, and preferable to others.

Mo Betta B-B-Q Tallahassee, FL

I got out of my car at *Mo Betta's* and was hit by a wave of hickory smoke flowing from a homemade smoker. "This is going to be good," I thought. I ordered the two-meat dinner special with two sides and sweet tea. I chose the ribs and brisket, with coleslaw and baked beans as sides. A piece of buttered bread came with the order. I tried the ribs first. The rub reminded me of *Southern Soul's* rub, sweet with a little heat. Unfortunately, the rib had little or no smoke ring. The pull was chewy. The brisket was served on a bun like a sandwich. It had a sweet sauce on it that tasted like any of the commercial sauces you can buy. The brisket was good, but had little smoke. It was cooked well, but tasted more like pot roast, it would have been mo' better if it had been seasoned more. The coleslaw was sweet but otherwise bland. The beans were good, seasoned well with a Tex-Mex taste. The sweet tea was good. All in all, with a little better seasoning, their brisket could be a winner.

Willie Jewell's Bar-B-Q Tallahassee, FL

Named after Willie Jewell Daniels, a Jacksonville native, the Tallahassee restaurant is one of many in their growing chain of stores. I visited at lunch time and told the helpful lady at the counter of my barbecue quest. She suggested the three-meat plate, so I ordered pulled pork, turkey, and ribs. Sides were mac and cheese, greens, and a complimentary cup of Brunswick stew. All was washed down with sweet tea. They offer a variety of sauces, I tried the gold and the sweet, both were good. The turkey was well cooked with a good smoke flavor, as was the pulled pork. The ribs had a smoke ring, but no flavor. They looked like they had been boiled first. The mac and cheese was doused in Velveeta cheese and not good. The greens were undercooked. The Brunswick stew however, was very good. Not a bad barbecue entry for Tallahassee.

The Red Shed Tallahassee, FL

The Red Shed looks like a good place to go eat barbecue and listen to music. The lady at the counter was friendly and helpful with my order. I got ribs, chicken wings (both sweet and spicy), and pulled pork. For side's I ordered mac and cheese, baked beans, and sweet tea to wash it all down. The wings and the ribs had a good rub that was a little bit of heat and sweet. The wings were excellent, some of the best I have had. They had a crispy skin and smoke flavor throughout. The ribs were fall off the bone, but only because they were overcooked, which was disappointing. The pulled pork had a good smoke flavor. They offer six varieties of sauce. I tried the sweet root beer, the 50/50, and the Red Shed. The 50/50 was the best, but none of them really go with pork. A vinegar or mustard sauce would have been better. The mac and cheese was full of cheese and flavor. The beans were a little hard and under cooked. The sweet tea was spot on. All in all, it was a good meal, save for the ribs.

Dreamland BBQ Tallahassee, FL
For a review, please look under the Alabama section.

NINE   MY STORY

I do not consider myself a barbecue novice. I have been smoking and grilling meat for the past forty years. My family would turn up their noses at a Thanksgiving turkey that had not been smoked to perfection. To even think about cooking meat in the oven would be considered sacrilege. When I speak of barbecue I am talking of *meat cooked low and slow, over indirect heat created by wood, where the meat is infused with the flavor of the wood used*.

I had started years ago with a Brinkman charcoal smoker augmented with hickory chunks and a water pan. It worked well, but I soon tired of having to keep it supplied with briquettes. I discovered an electric element that one could add to the smoker that solved this problem. For many years the Brinkman served me faithfully. I produced golden brown, juicy feasts of chicken, ribs and turkey with an occasional brisket. I wore out two smokers and elements through the years and was well one the way to retiring another, when I decided it was time to move up to the "real deal," a stick- burner smoker. For the uninitiated, this is a smoker that cooks with wood and has an off-set fire box. The meat is cooked by indirect heat while being smothered with the delicious aromas of the wood smoke.

Because barbecue has been a passion for so many years I had augmented my interest by reading books and watching television shows about barbecue places on television. Shows like *Diners, Dives, and Drive-Ins*, *Barbecue Pit-Masters, and Man, Fire, Food*, to name a few. I followed some favorite Pit-Masters and enjoyed watching the competitions. I also picked up a few pointers from the pros. To be honest, it was my wife who finally convinced me to make the leap. I had been "dream" shopping for smokers for a couple of years. but I was hesitant to pull the trigger on the purchase. It was not the money, but the commitment that made me hold back. Did I really want to get into barbecue big time? I hemmed and hawed to the point that my wife started looking for a smoker for me. Here's a tip to those guys that want something so bad you can taste it-- if your wife is for it, it's going to happen!

We were on a trip to Virginia and were driving on I-95 just north of Jacksonville, FL when a pick-up truck pulling a trailer load of *Lang* smokers passed. My wife pointed and said, "There's a smoker for you!" She even looked up the business on her iPhone. I mumbled something like "Yeah, they look nice." She looked at me again and said, " You need to go to that place, those look like some good smokers." We continued our trip and I did not mention the smoker to her the whole week we were gone. I did however check out the Lang website.

Ben Lang, the builder of the smokers, touted his "reverse flow" smokers that channeled the smoke over the meat twice while it cooked. First, when the smoke enters the cook chamber, and then again as it exited the chamber. He offered smokers of different sizes and combinations of smokers with a grill and/or a warmer box. You could get one on a trailer, or on small cart, depending on your need. Each was made to order at his business in Nahunta, Ga.

The next week when returning home, I decided to stop at Lang's and check out the smokers. It was love at first sight. I was like a kid in a candy store. There were smokers of all shapes and designs. Did I want one that could smoke in volume like the 84' smokers, or the 36' grill and smoker combo? Did I want one on a trailer to take around and cook at events, or one set up for backyard cooking? The choices seemed endless. I saw in my future mounds of smoked barbecue meats. All I needed to do was choose one. I decided to get a *Lang 36' Hybrid* that had two chambers, one for smoking and one for grilling—the best of both worlds. I also decided to have it mounted on a trailer I could pull behind my truck—envisioning church cookouts and barbecues at friend's homes. I put in my order and Ben told me it would be a month before I could come pick it up. I returned home thanking God because I knew He too loved the sweet aroma of barbecue—He even said so when He chose Able's meat offering instead of the vegetarian meal that Cain had offered.

Back home, I perused the Lang Smoker site studying its cooking tips and other helpful information, preparing myself to learn how an off-set "stick burner" worked. It was there that I saw an advertisement for an upcoming Lang "*Q-School*," taught by professional Pit- Master's. I noticed the dates would coincide with the time my smoker would be built and ready for pick-up. I called Lang's and after making sure the smoker would be ready that weekend, I signed my son Sam and myself up for the class.

Lang's "*Q-School*" was developed to instruct purchasers on how to properly use his smokers as well as give tips for those who wanted to cook for home or competition. Our class was offered as a one or two-day event. We decided to do the one-day event which covered competition cooking of brisket, chicken and ribs. It was taught by Lynnae Beth Oxley. She has her own business called *Sugar's BBQ* out of Portland Oregon. She was assisted by Steve Smith, a Florida boy who is with the *Blazin' 7's BBQ* cook team out of Inverness, Fl. Both are award winning Pit-Master's.

We arrived at the Lang cook house in Nahunta, Ga and were welcomed by Ben Lang and his wife, and pit masters Lynnae, and Steve. To get the day started they served us some local *Carroll's* sausage, cooked that morning. Our class consisted of 16 people from all over the United States who had bought a Lang and wanted to learn some pointers from the pro's. During the day Lynnae and Steve showed us how to prepare chicken thighs, ribs, and briskets, adding in special tips on trimming the meat, different types of rubs, injections, and how to prepare presentation boxes for the judges.

The meats were cooked on a *Lang* and Ben gave us some tips on maintaining the temperature, types of wood, and cooking temperatures for different meats. For those who were picking up a smoker, he offered to show us how to break it in for our first cook, even offering to do it while we attended the class. Basically, the smoker had to be tempered like you would a cast iron skillet. He suggested rubbing the interior area down with lard then firing up the grill to a high temperature and allowing the lard to seal the smoker. Sam and I chose to wait until we got our smoker home to do this, but some took him up on the offer. At the end of the day the class got to enjoy some of the best barbecue you can get, cooked on a *Lang*.

We tasted beautifully cooked chicken thighs, tender with bite through skin, and tasty ribs and brisket cooked to perfection. Sam and I came away with helpful information on how to use our smoker, plus a chance to eat some good food and meet some "brother's in barbecue."

My Lang 36 Hybrid

We towed the smoker home, showing it off first to Sam's wife, then mine. We decided to temper it the next day. It was only that night when I went to the grocery store that I found out that pure lard is not a common shelf stocker in Tallahassee, Fl. After some searching I found some lard bricks at the Winn Dixie. The next day I rubbed down my smoker and fired it up to 350 degrees. Smoke poured out of the chimney and the fire roared as the lard melted into the pores of the smoker. It was exciting to see the smoker in action, but disappointing that I could not cook on it until it was tempered. Ben had instructed us to let it temper then to clean the smoker by spraying a stream of water inside on the grills, sides and bottom while it was still hot, to remove any residue. The water hitting the intense heat would cause it to steam-clean and seal the pores. This process is to be repeated every time after a cook. It helps to keep the smoker clean, and remove any fat that could become rancid and affect the smoking process.

With the smoker properly tempered, we began trying different meats. We experimented with sweet and spicy rubs on ribs, injections in pork butts, fresh or "green" hams, chicken wings, and turkey breasts. All came out delicious, and each time we learned a little more on what flavor profile we liked, cooking times, temperatures, fire management, and meat preparations.

Sam bought me a book by Arron Franklin called *"Franklin Barbecue, A Meat-Smoking Manifesto."* In the book, Aaron Franklin lays out the basics of cooking barbecue. He starts with the type of smokers, different woods and their properties, how fire and smoke affect the cook, the meat used, the cook itself, and finishes with eating. *It is without a doubt one of the best books I have ever read on barbecue basics*. He does not try to fill his book up with recipes or self-promotion. He just wants to share his knowledge of how to make great barbecue. With this knowledge in hand, I soon became a connoisseur of meats and wood. I choose sweet favored hardwoods like cherry, and pecan to add their aromas to the meats. The old standbys of hickory and oak soon began filling an ever-growing wood-pile in my backyard. I searched for fresh cut trees left on the side of the road and hurried to beat the trash collectors to prized pieces of wood to use for cooking. I looked for the best cuts of meats, paying attention to "shiners" on ribs, and the fat marbling in briskets.

It did not take long to develop a taste for what real barbecue really is—meat slow cooked over wood. Not that stuff cooked in the "Easy Bake" oven type smokers augmented by pressed wood pellets or electric smokers, but true honest-to-God wood fired barbecue. By the summer of 2017 I had graduated from my Lang 36 to a Lang 60 on a wagon wheel cart. It you want a good smoker, you can't go wrong with a Lang.

My Lang 60

TEN   STICK A FORK IN IT, WE ARE DONE!

Our 16-day adventure took us to 15 states, traveling 12,100 miles, and eating in over 50 barbecue restaurants. After two great summers of barbecue, we returned home to mull over the different types of barbecue we had eaten. We still agreed it comes down to the meat. Those restaurants that use excessive sauce, while they create a flavorful meal, are hiding poorly cooked meat. Good barbecue takes time. Sometimes when a restaurant becomes successful, they begin to cut corners to handle demand. That might be in the cut of meat they buy, the length of time they cook, how the meat is cooked, or the wood they use. One thing any restaurant should remember… your reputation is only as good as the last plate you served.

Many barbecue restaurants today don't cook with wood like the old timers did. They use wood pellets in specially designed smokers to turn out the meat quickly. I am not knocking what they do, it's a business and they have to meet the demand. Many of them do this quite well. But is that *really* barbecuing? I suggest that when considering a barbecue restaurant, drive around back and see if they have a real wood pile and a pit. *That* is the real deal.

There are some that cook with wood that put out a fair product. It is only when you have compared them with others that you can tell the difference. That is one thing we learned on our trip. To the novice, and we met many as we traveled, *anything* cooked with wood is "*the best they ever had.*" That is understandable when you consider most are used to eating grilled meat and calling it barbecue. When they taste something that has that real smoke flavor, it blows their minds.

*Slow cooking meat with indirect heat from the coals of a wood fire that infuses the meat with the flavor of its rendered fat and the smoke, is **real** barbecue!*

The Men and the Meat

KENT

SAM

Kent's Top 30 BBQ Places

" ANYONE CAN PUT THE HEAT 2 THE MEAT BUT ONLY A FEW CAN BAR-B-Q"

1. Franklin's
2. Smitty's
3. Sam Jones
4. Skylight Inn
5. Wilbur's
6. Payne's
7. Danny Edward's
8. B's Crackling
9. Bums
10. Stiles Switch
11. B & B Lawnside
12. Fox Brother's
13. A & R
14. S.L.A.P.S.
15. Kruez's
16. Black's
17. Community Q
18. Sand Fly
19. Bonfire
20. Sweatman's
21. Scotts Variety
22. Miss Myra's
23. Big Bob Gibson
24. Arthur Bryant's
25. Home Team
26. Q39
27. Rendezvous
28. Oklahoma Joe's BBQ
29. Southern Soul
30. Jenkins Quality BBQ

Places with the Best:

Brisket
Franklin's
Smitty's
Stiles Switch
Danny Edward's (Burnt ends)
Kruez's
Black's
Moonies
Community Q
B's Crackling
Home Team
Sand Fly

Pork / Sandwich
Wilbur's
Payne's
B's Crackling
Skylight
A&R
Fox Brother's
Danny Edward's
Sam Jones
Stiles Switch
S.L.A.P.S.
Miss Myra's
Bonfire
Moonies
Community Q
Arthur Bryant's
Hite's
Bessinger's

Ribs
Franklin's
B's Cracklin'
B & B Lawnside

Bonfire
Smitty's
Blacks
S.L.A.P.S.
Payne's
Stiles Switch
Dreamland
Miss Myra's
Interstate
Big Bob's
Arthur Bryant's
Rendezvous
Jenkins Quality BBQ
Oklahoma Joe's BBQ
Old Brick Pit
Sand Fly

Chicken
Big Bob's
Miss Myra's
Bob Sykes
B's Cracklin
Dreamland

Whole Hog
Bums
Wilbur's
Skylight
Sam Jones
Sweatman's
Hite's

Sauces
Sprayberry's
Bessinger's
Home Team
Moonies
Sand Fly

Turkey
Franklin's
Stiles Switch
Willie Jewell's

Pits
Smitty's
Kurez's
Sam Jones
Wilbur's
Skylight
Bums
Hite's
Sweatman's
Scotts Variety
Payne's
Rendezvous

Desserts
Franklin's –Pies (from Cake and Spoon)
B-B's Lawnside- Bread Pudding
B's Cracklin'-- Banana Pudding & Peach Crisp
Stiles Switch—Banana Pudding
Jenkins- Red Velvet Cake
Bob Sykes- Lemon Pie & Red Velvet Cake
Miss Myra's- Banana pudding & Homemade Pies

Sides
Fox Brothers- Mac & Cheese
B's Crackling- Collards, Mac & Cheese, Cornbread
Mo Betta- Baked Beans
Dreamland- Okra, Coleslaw
Bonfire- Collards, Baked Beans
Community Q- Mac & Cheese
Sonny's- Beans, Corn Nuggets
Payne's- Slaw
Willie Jewel's- Brunswick Stew

Wings
Fox Brothers
Bonfire
Q39
The Red Shed

100 BBQ Places You Should Try
(**Bold** denotes ones we visited)

Alabama

Big Bob Gibson's 1715 6th Ave, Decatur
Dreamland Bar-B-Que, 5535 15th Ave E, Tuscaloosa
Bob Sykes Bar-B-Q, 1724 9th Ave N, Bessemer
Miss Myra's Pit Bar-B-Q, 3278 Cahaba Heights Rd, Vestavia
Carlisle's 3511 6th Avenue, Birmingham
Full Moon Bar-B-Que 525 25th St. South, Birmingham
Big Daddy's Real Pit Bar-B-Que, 205 N Rawls St, Enterprise,
Top Hat Barbecue 8725 US Hwy 31, Blount Springs,
Leo & Susie's Green Top BBQ 7530 Hwy 78, Dora
Golden Rule BBQ 2506 Crestwood Blvd, Irondale
Saw's BBQ, 1008 Oxmoor Rd, Homewood
Archibald's 1211MLK Jr. Blvd, Northport
Pruett's BBQ 1617 Rainbow Dr., Gadsden
Phil's BBQ 534 Randolph Ave., Eufaula

Georgia

Fox Brothers 1238 Delkab Ave, Atlanta
Sprayberry's Barbecue 229 Jackson Street, Newnan,
Old Brick Pit Barbeque 4805 Peachtree Road, Atlanta
Sand Fly BBQ 1220 Barnard St., Savannah
B's Cracklin' 12409 White Bluff Rd., Savannah
Southern Soul 2020 Demere Rd., St. Simons Island
Moonies Texas BBQ 5545 Atlanta Hwy., Flowery Branch
Community Q Barbeque 1361 Clairmont Rd, Decatur
Heirloom Market BBQ 2243 Akers Mill Road, Atlanta
Wiley's Championship BBQ 4700 US-80, Savannah
Fat Mac's BBQ 1811 Piedmont Rd, NE Atlanta
Pit Boss BBQ 856 Virginia Ave, Atlanta
Anna's BBQ 1976 Hosea L. Williams Dr., Atlanta
Big Shanty Smokehouse 3393 Cherokee St NW, Kennesaw,
Papa Buck's BBQ - 1085 S Lewis St, Metter
Williamson Bros Bar-B-Q - 1425 Roswell Rd, Marietta
Fresh Air Barbecue 1164 Highway 42 South, Jackson
The Wicked Pig 151 Main St., Clayton
The Happy Hog BBQ 1586 Highway 76 W. Hiawassee

North Carolina

Skylight Inn 4618 S. Lee St., Ayden
Sam Jones 715 W. Firetower Rd., Winterville

103

Bum's 566 E. 3rd St., Ayden
B's Barbecue, 751 B's Barbecue Road, Greenville
Wilbur's Barbecue 4172 US-70, Goldsboro
Bonfire Barbecue 1056 Patton Avenue West, Ashville
Red Bridges BBQ Lodge 2000 E Dixon Blvd, Shelby
Jack Cobb & Son Barbecue Place 3883 S. Main St., Farmville
Barbeque Center 900 N Main St, Lexington
Lexington Barbecue 100 Smokehouse Lane, Lexington
Cook's Barbecue 366 Valiant Drive, Lexington
Tarheel Q. BBQ 6835 US-64, Lexington
Smiley's BBQ 917 Winston Rd, Lexington
Short Sugar's 1328 S Scales St, Reidsville
Keaton's BBQ 17365 Cool Springs Rd, Cleveland
Allen & Son BBQ 5650 US 15-501, Pittsboro
Grady's Barbecue 3096 Arrington Bridge Rd., Dudley
Parker's Barbecue 3109 Memorial Drive, Greenville
Moore's Old Tyme Barbeque 3711 MLK, Jr. Blvd, New Bern
Luella's Bar-B-Que 501 Merrimon Ave., Asheville
Thig's BBQ House 1722 Catherine Lake Rd., Jacksonville
Little Pig's 226 Brookdale Dr., Statesville

South Carolina

Hite's Bar-B-Que 240 Dreher Rd, West Columbia
Scotts Variety BBQ 2734 Hemingway Hwy, Hemingway
Sweatman's BBQ 1427 Eutaw Rd, Holly Hill
Henry's Smokehouse 240 Wade Hampton Blvd Greenville,
Fiery Ron's Home Team BBQ 126 Williman St. Charleston
Bessinger's 1602 Savannah Hwy, Charleston
Cannon's BBQ 1903 Nursery Road Little Mountain
Lewis Barbecue 464 North Nassau St., Charleston
Brown's Bar-B-Que 809 N. Williamsburg County Hwy., Kingstree
Hite's Barbecue 467 Church St. Batesburg-Leesville

Memphis, Tennessee

A & R 1802 Elvis Presley Blvd.
Payne's 1762 Lamar Ave
Jim Neely's Interstate Bar-B- Que 2265 SE 3rd St.
Charlie Vergo's Rendezvous 52 S. 2nd St.
Central BBQ 147 East Butler Ave
Corky's BBQ 5259 Poplar Ave
The BBQ Shop 1782 Madison Ave
Bozo's Hot Pit BBQ 342 Hwy 70 W., Mason, Tenn.

Kansas City, Missouri

Q 39 1000 W 39th St.
Danny Edwards Boulevard BBQ 2900 Southwest Blvd.
Gates 1221 Brooklyn Ave.
Oklahoma Joe's 3002 W. 47th St.
Arthur Bryant's 1727 Brooklyn Ave.
S.L.A.P.S. 553 Central Ave.
B-B Lawnside BBQ 1205 E. 85th St.
Jack Stack Barbecue 101 W 22nd St. #300
LC's Barbecue 5800 Blue Parkway
Winslow's BBQ 20 E. 5th St.

Texas

Franklin BBQ 900 E. 11th, Austin
Stiles Switch BBQ & Brew 6610 North Lamar Blvd, Austin
Smitty's 208 S. Commerce St., Lockhart
Black's 215 N. Main, Lockhart
Kruez's 619 N. Colorado, Lockhart
John Mueller Meat Co. 2500 E. 6th St., Austin
La Barbeque 1906 E. Cesar Chavez St., Austin
Lamberts Downtown Barbecue 401 W. 2nd St, Austin

Florida

Jenkins BBQ 830 N. Pearl Street, Jacksonville
Sonny's BBQ 1460 Timberlane Rd., Tallahassee
Mission BBQ 261 S. Magnolia Dr., Tallahassee
Mo' Betta Bar-B-Que 3105 Apalachee Pkwy., Tallahassee
Jim & Milts Bar-B-Q 1923 W. Pensacola St., Tallahassee
4 Rivers Smokehouse 1817 Thomasville Rd., Tallahassee
The Red Shed 3031 Crump Rd., Tallahassee
Willie Jewel's BBQ 5442 Thomasville Rd., Tallahassee
Blazing 7's BBQ 111 N. Florida Ave., Inverness

Suggested Books for Barbecue Addicts

"*Franklin Barbecue, A Meat-Smoking Manifesto*" by Aaron Franklin

"*Smokestack Lightening*" by Lolis Eric Elie

"*The One True Barbecue*" by Rien Fertel

"*Hog Heaven a Guide to South Carolina Barbecue*" by Allie Patricia Wall and Ron L. Layne

"*Weber's Smoke*" by Jamie Purviance

"*Pitmaster*" by Andy Husbands and Chris Hart

"*Project Smoke*" by Steven Raichlen

"*The South's Best Butts*" by Matt Moore

"*Barbecue, The History of an American Institution*" by Robert F. Moss

"*The Passion of Barbecue*" by The Kansas City Barbecue Association

"*The Easy Art of Smoking Food*" by Chris Dubbs and Dave Heberle

"*Southern Food*" by John Egerton

"**Real Barbecue**" by Vince Staten & Greg Johnson

"**Barbecue Crossroads**" by Robb Walsh

OTHER BOOKS BY J. KENT THOMPSON

Remembering Florida's Forgotten Coast

The Florida Seafood Cookbook

The History of Florida's Fisher's and Enforcer's

Old Time Tallahassee From A to Z

North Florida Roads with Stories on the Side

All are available at lulu.com, Barnes and Nobles, or Amazon